POLISHED

HOW NAIL SALONS SAVED VIETNAMESE-AMERICANS

T0061954

BI AYERS

POLISHED

BI AYERS

www.BookpressPublishing.com

Published in Des Moines, Iowa, by:

BookPress Publishing
P.O. Box 71532, Des Moines, IA 50325
www.BookpressPublishing.com

Publisher's Cataloging-in-Publication Data

Names: Ayers, Bi, author.
Title: Polished : How nail salons saved Vietnamese-Americans / Bi Ayers.
Description: Includes bibliographical references. |
Des Moines, IA: Bookpress Publishing, 2023.
Identifiers: LCCN: 2022910545 | ISBN: 978-1-947305-45-8
Subjects: LCSH Ayers, Bi. | Vietnamese Americans--Biography. | Entrepreneurs--Biography. | Vietnamese American business enterprises--United States. | Success in business--United States. | Manicuring. | Beauty shops. | BISAC BIOGRAPHY & AUTOBIOGRAPHY / Business | BIOGRAPHY & AUTOBIOGRAPHY / Cultural, Ethnic & Regional / Asian & Asian American | BIOGRAPHY & AUTOBIOGRAPHY / Personal Memoirs
Classification: LCC HD2346.U5 .A94 2023 | DDC 338/.04/0899592073—dc23

First Edition
Printed in the United States of America
10 9 8 7 6 5 4 3 2 1

This book is dedicated to my wife, Anh,
who has always been supportive of everything I do.

CONTENTS

ACKNOWLEDGEMENTS

I would like to acknowledge our precious kids, Kelsie, Sylvia, and Eva for enduring our hectic work schedule; my parents, Doug and Duong, for their support, encouragement, and for nurturing my ability; the ProNails Spa team for their hard work, their trust in me, their continuing effort to build a great team, and for working to create a great salon; our clients because none of this would have been possible without them, their trust, their promotion, and their enthusiasm which makes our day more enjoyable—and as our slogan says, we truly enjoy your presence.

PART 1

The Real Story Behind this $7 Billion Industry and its Connection to Vietnamese Culture

Who would have thought that the art of nails could save lives? Did you ever think getting a manicure would make a life-changing difference for an entire culture? If you have visited a nail salon, you can count yourself as a contributor to the growth and success of a business that has become a way of life for many Americans.

There are hundreds of thousands of different businesses in the US today, but when you think of industries that save lives, what first comes to mind? Medicine? Philanthropy?

How about nail salons? Believe it or not, the nail salon industry not only saved the lives of thousands, but since its inception in America in the early 1900s, it has grown into an industry valued at more than $7 billion. This industry increased diversity in America, drawing Vietnamese families in particular, who later made many significant contributions that continue to help our country grow and thrive today.

According to a 2018 article in the *International Focus Houston Magazine*,[1] Vietnamese culture has made many notable contributions to American life. Consider engineer Dinh Truon Han, who in 2006 won an environmental award from the White House and was selected as one of America's fifty most influential American leaders by *Public Works Magazine*. Or take Dr. Huynh Phuoc Duong, a professor at the UCLA Davis Geffen School of Medicine, who founded the Social Assistance Programme For Viet Nam, or SAP-VN. Or how about Trung Dung, a Vietnamese-American who arrived in the US in 1985 with two dollars in his pocket and in fifteen years had earned $1.8 billion from the sale of his OnDisplay company to Vignette Corp? He now works as managing director of V-Home Group, a company that connects Vietnamese-American businesspeople to investment opportunities in Viet Nam. Finally, the magazine mentions Ms. Le Duy Loan, who was the first woman and Asian elected Senior Fellow at Texas Instruments.

According to *International Focus Houston*, in 1990, Vietnamese-American intellectuals established the Viet Nam Science and Culture Association, a non-profit focused on the preservation of Vietnamese culture and leadership through educational assistance for young Vietnamese-Americans. The association now has divisions in Austin, Dallas, Toronto, and Washington. Any foodie will recognize the delicious cuisine the Vietnamese have contributed to American culture—the warm, spicy rice noodle soup called pho, egg rolls, fried fish, braised fish, braised chicken with lemongrass, sweet and sour spare ribs, and stir-fired beef to name a few. But Vietnamese-Americans have preserved their culture and traditions not only through cuisine, but also through language education, family values like a deep respect for elders and good parenting practices, emphasizing traditional dress during special occasions, and veneration for the dead.

The booming nail salon industry has a unique beginning which might be one of the best-kept secrets in America. It not only created demand for a new service, but an opportunity for a diverse, hard-working culture that needed to start over. This industry has a story that I want to share because I'm a proud participant in it. Why is the nail salon industry so special? Because it was developed through historical partnerships between countries, cultural exchanges, and acceptance, a value that from my perspective symbolizes what America is all about. It's important to me because my Vietnamese heritage played a critical role in developing this industry, and it continues to do that today.

In this book, I'm going to give you a look inside this amazing industry that has saved lives and provided opportunities to people in need of a fresh start. I'm going to show you how and why the Vietnamese, my people, came to dominate it, and trace its origins back to the entertainment industry. I'm going to demonstrate how one significant group played a major role in building nail salons into an empire valued at **more than $7 billion**!

I'll also tell you my story of leaving Viet Nam when I was fifteen and starting all over in a new country in which I couldn't communicate. I've experienced both victory and defeat in life, and my story and this book will offer you a perspective you have never heard before.

Get ready to read real, untold stories about Vietnamese heritage and the stigma behind the business, along with my secrets to success, and I'll show you how my culture and life have allowed me to excel in this country and this industry. Consider it an entertaining tale with a history lesson and a bit of training to help you become successful in your own life and business.

Welcome to the secrets of the nail salon.

MY STORY

Let me take you on a walk in someone else's shoes. Someone you wouldn't normally think about. Picture this. You're a fifteen-year-old in Viet Nam. You just finished swimming in the famous Perfume River that divides the country in two. It's massive in size, but that never stopped you or the dozen neighborhood kids you're friends with from jumping off rocks and swinging from ropes into the breathtakingly cool water. There are many of you and few things to worry about. At the end of the day, you say goodbye and turn to go home in your wet swim clothes because you have nothing else. They head to their homes, too, but unlike the others, yours has a steel gate out front that leads into a courtyard with tile walkways lined with white flowers on either side. The walls are a drab color, and you can still see gouges and holes in them from bullets and bomb fragments. You approach the front entry, grand compared to other homes, and with your hand on the railing, walk up the few concrete steps that narrow toward the top, beckoning you toward French doors. This edifice is very different and larger than the other connected homes in your neighborhood.

The smell of fresh noodles hanging in the air invites you in, and you find your grandmother and mother hard at work in the kitchen with the dirt floor. They are both petite women, but neither are strangers to hard work nor providing food for your large family. You find your uncles all sitting in the big courtyard, talking business. They all live together as it's normal to have multiple generations under one roof. Your three-bedroom ranch home is far more desirable than the home of any neighbor for many blocks. This tends to be a problem under a socialist government, but your grandfather and uncles were smart enough to take care of that. They used the 100 tons of copper your grandfather had buried in the back yard as leverage, giving it up to keep the house. You enter the living room, the only place in the house with a tile floor, and find your grandfather sitting alone, reading. He is well-respected, the man of the house, but also a man of few words.

Your grandfather is an official for the French Colonial Empire, and you come from a long line of business-minded family members. They understand how things work in this socialist society. At any time, the government could come in and take over any home they wanted or take possession of any belongings you have—your business, your property, your vehicles, and any assets you have. It's something your family learned generations ago. They've seen plenty of turmoil and became proactive to survive. Many things happened in your country before you were born, but you learn more about this each morning while you sit with your grandfather and listen to stories from his life over the aroma of his tobacco pipe and your cup of fresh-brewed tea. Unlike other kids, you look forward to learning more about your family history. Though a quiet man, he is willing to tell you stories of the past, which makes you feel special. Like your mother, your grandfather finds ways to put you into a Catholic school with private tutors where you learn piano, French, and more, even though he is financially poor. It's his way of showing a little favoritism.

All things considered, you know your family is doing well looking after you and that your home is a safe place to go. You don't have much, and there is always chaos in the house because so many are living there, but it's what you know. You expect to continue living there, and you've been going to school for a while, but soon it's time to con-sider quitting school to find a job. You have more opportunity than most, but it still weighs on your mind as a fifteen-year-old because you know the days of playing with the neighborhood kids in the river are numbered.

You go back inside, and your mother ushers you over to a private area. She proceeds to tell you that she is going to marry the American soldier who has been visiting. He completed five consecutive tours during the Viet Nam war and made a positive impression on you and your family. You like this American soldier because he has visited often and has brought presents from the US that you could never get in Viet Nam, but his marriage to your mother means your life will change completely.

So what do you do?

As you can guess, yes, this was my life.

I don't tell you this to ask for your sympathy or gratitude, but rather to tell you that there are many in my culture who have had similar experiences, some easier, some much harder. But to give you the full perspective, I want you to understand that many Vietnamese-Americans have experienced a story strikingly similar to mine, especially those who were young in the mid-1970s.

I was born in a small town in central Viet Nam called Hue, also known as the Imperial City, which was once the capitol of Viet Nam for almost 150 years during the reign of the Nguyen Dynasty. Hue is situated about sixty miles south of where the Demilitarized Zone (DMZ) was during the Viet Nam War, and it's well-known as the site of the 1968 Tet Offensive, a battle where the US Marines and South Vietnamese soldiers fought fiercely for many days to gain control of the city. You could say it's a small town with a Midwestern vibe, but the weather is just like Seattle's—hot summer days and constant winter rains. The trees and foliage are green and full of life. Some describe Hue as poetic, romantic, or dreamy, full of UNESCO heritage preservation sites with lots of architectural history, pagodas, and the citadel. For a kid, it was a good place to be—empty streets with hardly any cars because those with the privilege were either government officials or people of power, lots of green space to explore, where I often played games of soccer with my friends and swam to cool off.

My life now is a far cry from my teenage years, but I don't mean this in the sense of age. I mean that Viet Nam is a completely different story.

Life in Viet Nam is simple but hard, and at that time, opportunities were few and far between for anyone looking to improve their career or social status. My determination to succeed in life was supported by my family, especially my grandmother, Nguyen Thi Ty, but I normally called her Ba Ngoai (maternal grandma). She was small and caring, with a big heart and an education no higher than second grade, but she smoothly ran family business, and some say she could do simple math in her head faster than a calculator.

My grandmother knew a different life than I did. She lived through Viet Nam's many governmental changes—French colonialism, democracy, socialism. She found herself running away from socialism. She was only able to enjoy democracy for a short time, and it's the government I often heard the most about from her while we lived under socialist control.

My grandma in 2003.

My grandparents originally came from a province in North Viet Nam called Hai Phong, where Grandpa was an official for the French Colonial Empire and a landowner. Life was good until the revolutionary group called the Viet

Minh enforced land reform by confiscating land from large landlords and rich peasants. They also severely punished the wealthy and foreign sympathizers through persecution, decapitation, live burials, beatings, confiscation of property, internment in labor camps supporting guerillas, and the abduction of sons older than 12 for enlistment in military service. In 1954, my grandma was visiting her family in a small village called Ha Dong. While there, she witnessed the brutality of the Viet Minh's land reform policy, and it did not resemble their revolutionary pitch or their propaganda. People were being traumatized and killed for no reason. Their land was taken away from them. Families were being torn apart as the government incentivized people to rat out each other in the spirit of socializing wealth and for the cause of the revolution. She recognized the danger of staying in Hai Phong and encouraged grandpa to emigrate to South Viet Nam. The border would be closed soon, and after that, getting caught while attempting to cross to freedom could mean death.

Viet Nam was divided under the 1954 Geneva Convention Agreement in the effort to keep the French out of North Viet Nam. Everything north of the thirty-ninth parallel would be controlled by the communist government, and everything south would be governed by the newly formed Democratic Republic of Viet Nam. Having not witnessed the violence first-hand, Grandpa wasn't easily convinced, but she knew that should they stay, simply the title he'd once held in the former regime could mean his death. She had a plan that she knew would eventually convince Grandpa to cross the border.

She told him that if he didn't go, she would take their son and go to Sai Gon by themselves. He didn't think she was serious, but he knew where she would be if he needed to find her—

My grandpa prior to 1975.

there was only one family they knew living in Sai Gon at the time. She waited for a short time without any response from Grandpa, then snuck out before daylight one morning, telling no one her plan. She was defecting toward a newly formed democratic government. In the next few days, finally accepting the truth that Grandma was serious, Grandpa packed up and boarded the last US ship docked at the port of Hai Phong, heading south.

"Sai Gon was vibrant and much more westernized," Grandma said every time I asked her to tell me the story, usually before bedtime. They had to adjust to the new environment and mostly unfamiliar culture as most of the south had been influenced by the French, who had colonized Viet Nam for nearly a century. My grandparents quickly realized they were in a different world and wasted no time in search for the right opportunity that fit their entrepreneurial spirit. After some time of moving around, they settled in Hue, a much smaller city than Sai Gon with many opportunities for selling coal. Competition was minimal in that area.

The success of the coal business opened doors to other opportunities, and eventually, they got into the business of selling copper. During the war, copper was plentiful in weapons technology, so they collected ammunition casings and bomb shells, though removing the resource for sale was not an easy task. The process can be dangerous as many bombs and shell casings were found undetonated, she told me. Once the copper was ready, they sold to the highest bidder, typically either the Americans or the Japanese. Their hard work and optimism helped them build a little business empire and earned them status among the city elites.

They were entrepreneurs with great motivation and an interest in business. They seemed to always run toward freedom and opportunity. My family was well-known in the city in the 1970s, but Viet Nam had changed into a war-torn country under the constant threat of communism. No one ever imagined that after the US forces withdrew, they would see the last days of freedom cherished in Viet Nam. April 30, 1975 is a day known in the west as "the Fall of South Viet Nam," but it's better-known as a National Resentment Day for those who lost their freedom and were forced to flee their home country or be put into a "re-education camp," known among the prisoners as a brainwash-and-torture camp.

After the Democratic Republic of South Viet Nam fell to North Vietnamese socialism, my family lost everything. It was illegal to have any wealth of your own, so your lives and daily activities were being monitored until they believed, beyond any reasonable doubt, that you no longer held any valuables. As business-minded people, my grandparents were strong enough to endure the change and adapt to the new government. You didn't have a voice in Viet Nam back then. I learned this and accepted it. I would do the best I could to help support my family.

As a child in this environment, I went to school, did my chores, and worked hard. I would often talk to my grandmother about the things I learned in school, and she would tell me stories that contradicted everything I learned, especially regarding the history of our country. Grandma would give her perspective of the history, which painted a tale of war, freedom, the abundance of food, and the opportunities she once experienced, which often differed from the lesson of the day; however, she made me promise not to tell. We would be in real danger if we discussed things contradictory to my education or criticized the current government. So I took my grandmother's words of wisdom and tucked them away for my own history lessons.

It wasn't until my teenage years that I was truly faced with a major change. My mother took me to a room away from the family to tell me she had decided to marry an American soldier. We would call him Lee, his middle name, because Doug would be too hard to pronounce. My first impression was that he was funny, loving, caring, strong, and fearless—kind of a John Wayne, if I'd known who that was at the time—and he was an explorer, too. Since 1994, when Viet Nam opened its doors to foreigners, he had traveled all over the country. Most foreigners at this time were hesitant to even come, but by the time I met him, he had traveled from the south end of the country to the north and had even visited places most Vietnamese had never heard of. I could say he made a good impression on our family. We all liked him. It's only a slight overstatement to say even the old North

Vietnamese Army Colonel's family living across the street liked him.

Doug Ayers had proposed to my mother and petitioned for her and I to live with him in this foreign country, the United States of America, where they spoke English, and worst of all, my extended family would not be joining us. My grandmother was to stay in Viet Nam.

I didn't want to go. I didn't want to leave the only place I'd ever known, where my aunts and uncles and cousins all lived. Now I had to move to a place where I couldn't understand anyone and leave my friends too. What was going on? I must confess, it didn't truly hit me until the morning we left. I said goodbye to all my friends and family in Hue to start completely over. As we landed in Sai Gon, I saw the biggest plane I'd ever seen—the one that would be taking us over the ocean. It wasn't like we were moving down the street; we were moving across the world, and it would be a very long time before I would see my family again.

Looking back on that memory, I can still hear my grandmother saying that I would have better opportunities in the US. I would have a better life. The sky was the limit for me. She knew living in a socialist system would prevent me from growing to my fullest potential, and dreams would be nothing more than figments of the imagination. She knew I could go further than middle school and could do better than finding any old vocation to make a living. She knew a democratic government would allow me to make my dreams a reality and achieve my goals. She had experienced it herself in the '60s and '70s, and even during the war.

She knew what I didn't know.

It took me a while, but I get it now. I live here where my success is based on how hard I work, and I don't have to bribe anyone for an opportunity. These are things I realized later, when I became accustomed to the culture and the way of life in the US.

When we landed in Los Angeles, I felt like I was stepping into a Hollywood movie set. Large buildings lined the sky, city lights peppered the darkness, and bridges and overpasses complemented by a perpetual traffic jam surrounded us. People crowded the sidewalks, and cars emitted a steady stream of honking as we made our way to our hotel. I gazed out of the car window, amazed at the view but missing home.

We spent the night in LA, then flew to Iowa, where my new hometown was Colo, population 984. It was ideal, looking back. Unlike LA, I wasn't lost in a crowd because there rarely was one in Colo, and the people who lived there were kind.

I started school, and it was nerve-wracking because I wasn't sure if I'd fit in. Would I be accepted and make friends with people I'd never met? Was I dressed appropriately? In Viet Nam, we all wore uniforms to school, so it didn't matter. As a kid, I wore whatever was given to me, whatever my family could afford. I knew nothing about the popular fashion brands like Nike or Adidas. I'd spend a large part of the day in English as a Second Language (ESL) class. I was on my own for the rest. Thankfully, my fellow students helped me. Math was the easiest subject because I understood numbers even when I didn't understand the language. I was the only Vietnamese kid in the entire school, so it was intimidating at first, but I made friends quickly. Many were curious about where I'd come from, and I think a few thought I knew the Karate Kid. I had no idea what they were talking about, but nonetheless, they helped me get established in the new American culture.

It was so different. I had the opportunity to learn as much as I wanted, and by the time my second semester of school came, I had made the honor roll, a status I maintained throughout my school years. My grandmother was right; America allowed me to dream of a bigger and better life than I could have had back in Viet Nam. I still miss my country and family back home, but here, I can do so much more. Unlike most Vietnamese-Americans, who go to college to chase destinies as scientists or doctors, I chose to pursue my passion for business. I wanted to be successful just like my family had been during the war. With the support of my grandmother, my mother, and everyone else, I was free to make it happen.

Before I met Doug, I didn't have a father for most of my life. Maybe that's why Grandpa always made me feel special—or maybe it was because I was his first grandson. I remember he would always wake me up early to accompany him to morning tea—a ritual involving listening to BBC radio, telling me stories, and offering me words of wisdom. Most kids at that age would've been bored out of their mind, but I enjoyed it. I enjoyed his stories, the tea, and the smell of his pipe tobacco. What I liked even more was his mid-afternoon snack time. He would often take me out for a snack and a stroll down the street, just the two of us. I felt very special and completely loved. I never felt like I was missing a father figure because of that connection. They gave me the love I needed, and I learned so many great life lessons from my grandpa.

That life wasn't as fulfilling as my life here, however. Moving to the US made me miss that time with my family, but Doug was a great father to me, and he turned out to be the perfect role model I needed as I was becoming a man. He was also a great mentor. He always pushed me in a positive way, testing my abilities, which made me a strong man. He saw potential in me, and I'm grateful for his encouragement. When people said I couldn't do something, Doug helped show me how I could. He taught me how to work hard and enjoy life. He took me fishing and hunting, taught me how to change oil and fix the car, how to repair a home, do plumbing, run electricity, and most importantly, he taught me to be responsible and to always put family first. As he always said, "Never get attached to anything except your family."

As a new kid in town, Doug also offered me new experiences. The first summer I was in the US, he got me a job that not many Midwesterners could get. I worked with Doug's friend on a ship in Cape Cod, and we fished for lobster during the early summer months. I was on the ocean all summer, and after lobster season, I boarded another ship with Doug's friend to hunt for treasure. Believe it or not, I was a real treasure hunter, and we saw so many things. I even caught a glimpse of the culture at Provincetown,

better known as P-town, on the north end of Cape Cod. I can
tell you, there is nothing like that culture in Viet Nam. The
entire summer was an educational experience and one I will
never forget.

I was fortunate to meet the
rest of Doug's siblings. They were
all friendly to me and treated me
like I had always been a part of
the family. Uncle Craig always
extended great encouragement
and words of wisdom to me. Aunt
Vicky invited us to ball games or
to go shopping to get us acquaint-

Me on the fishing boat in 1997.

ed with American culture. We often spent Thanksgiving at
Uncle Craig and Aunt Vicky's house, filling up on delicious
food and playing card games. I'm also grateful to have been
able to spend many Labor Day weekends at Uncle Lynn and
Aunt Dian's lake house at Lake Tapawingo, Missouri. This
family gathering featured swimming, fishing, boating, and
dining. They went above and beyond to wel-come us, and
even my Aunt Janet, who was a sweet, easygoing lady,
allowed me to live with her for a semester in college while I
looked for an apartment. These amazing people all had a
positive influence on me in some way.

Doug taught me work ethic and how to connect with
people. I used those lessons to help me work through my
summers, whether the job was washing cars at the local deal-
ership or excelling in school, but Doug's advice also got me
through life. I'm not afraid to work hard or to keep going

when life gets difficult. I just put my head down and plow through it. This attitude paid off when I graduated with honors and received a full scholarship to Iowa State University through the multi-cultural vision program.

College was an amazing experience, but not at all what I had expected. I didn't realize the freedom I would have, or the responsibility. I had a lot to learn about living on my own, but it taught me some very important lessons about how to go it alone. This was again completely different from Viet Nam, where family members always gave guidance.

With my foundation from childhood and the tools I learned in my new home, I was ready to fulfill my destiny. This readiness gave way to epiphany when I won two first-place trophies at the 2004 Mr. Iowa Body-Building Contest through the North American Natural Bodybuilding Feder-

Our first trip back to Viet Nam in 2002 standing in front of the famous "Hanoi Hilton" prison camp.

ation (NANBF). Training for something like that was no small task. It was a commitment that required hard discipline, mentally and physically. I worked out twice a day for an hour alongside my full-time college schedule. In this regimen, my days started at 5:30 a.m., and I had a strict diet. I pushed myself to the limit, and it paid off when I won. At that point, I knew that if I set my mind on something, I could do it. My grandmother was right.

OUR BUSINESS

Do you ever wonder about the story behind the people you meet? I hear these stories every day. People from all walks of life come into my business to escape for a moment of relaxation and camaraderie in an otherwise crazy, busy life. They sit in the chair across from me and smile, ready for their nails to be transformed into something beautiful. In the process, we talk about their kids, their grandchildren, the latest gossip, and the local forecast. When I'm done, they get up, admire my work, and thank me before returning to reality—their own busy lives full of to-do lists—and anticipate their return to our salon.

No matter where they come from, they have contributed to my business in exchange for a quality nail salon experience. I have a sense of fulfillment knowing I'm providing an outstanding service and making a difference in my own way. I'm the proud owner of ProNails Spa in Ames, Iowa, a business that has grown exponentially over the last ten years. You could say I'm a forty-year-old Vietnamese immigrant living the American dream. I have a wonderful wife and partner, three beautiful children, a mortgage, a business, and a Golden Retriever. Okay, I don't have a Golden Retriever, but I would say I have a fortunate life and home that I'm proud of.

I get up in the morning, grab a cup of tea before getting the kids off to school, then rush over to my nail salon where I work with amazing people every day and make new friends every few hours. As an owner and a husband, I take pride in knowing that at our nail salon, everyone knows who's in charge, who's the boss, who manages everything. That is, of course, my wife, Anh.

For those of you who are married, you can understand that she may be the boss at the nail salon, but at home, well, she's still the boss. "Happy wife, happy life" is a phrase I have learned to live by here in America.

HOW IT ALL STARTED

After college, I lived in Des Moines and then moved to Houston, Texas, where I worked for an engineering company. When Anh delivered our second child, we decided to move back to Iowa to raise our family.

Anh was a nail technician, and she was very good at it. We had talked about what we wanted to do when we settled in Iowa. I proposed the idea of opening our own nail salon because I saw an opportunity for a quality, professional service and a place where people could relax, reconnect, and not be rushed in and rushed out, like a fast-food joint.

Owning a nail salon was an easy decision but a hard one at the same time. Like many Vietnamese, we knew how to do nails and had many resources and connections due to our culture and network. Anh wasn't so enthused about the idea because we had never owned a business, and she knew running a business was easier said than done. This was an obstacle we recognized right away, but I had the passion and determination to own my own business, and we both wanted to move forward.

As small as Ames is, the town was saturated with nail salons, and Anh knew competing for market share was not going to be easy as our rivals were well-established. She also knew her broken English was a weakness and would rather not deal with the headache of handling difficult customers and managing technicians with different personalities. She worried about the kids, how to find enough time for them, prepare dinner each night, and help them with schoolwork. I assured her that our kids would always be our first priority, and that if we did this, I would take care of the business side while she would manage the salon. We knew this would be a big commitment since I was still working full-time at the engineering company, our lifeline until the business gained some traction. I was not confident in her commitment at the time, but little did I know, she was adventurous herself.

I would never say starting a business is easy, but having

worked for a young, successful company that valued process, procedure, and quality for eight years, I knew where to start. Ames is a small college town, but the research had shown it was and might still be one of the top ten most-educated cities in America, filled with wealth and a limitless supply of opportunity. I knew we must earn the trust of this demographic, primarily focusing on people in their thirties and older. We also knew there were always risks when opening a business regardless of the strength of our business plan or strategy.

As reported by Fundera, approximately twenty percent of businesses fail in the first year, and thirty percent fail in the second.[2] By the end of the fifth year, about half will fail, and by the end of the decade, only thirty percent of businesses survive, which totals a seventy percent failure rate in ten years on average. I guess you will have a chance of success if your business makes it past this statistical time frame, but getting there might not be as rosy as you might imagine. We didn't want to put all our eggs in the same basket, so we wanted to start out small with low initial investment and focus on serving our niche.

The success we have today is due to our continuing efforts to improve, the consistency in our service, and the hard work of our technicians. But we have also had to push through a lot of stress and tackle new issues every day.

In the early years, things were sometimes difficult as we tried to build a culture for our business, control quality, manage technicians, and work to please difficult clients. All of that was expected, but everyone has a breaking point. That point for Anh was about two years in, when she told me it was too stressful. She was exhausted, and we realized that neither of us has taken a vacation in the last two years except for the occasional day trip with the kids to water parks or someplace fun to spend more time with them. I knew things would improve, but we needed to balance our lives better. I could not allow her to continue fighting with the stress. After all, business is supposed to be fun, so I finally agreed to sell.

It was a tough decision to let go of something we had both worked so hard to build. I felt we were abandoning not only our business, but our technicians and clients as well. The technicians, who were committed to our team and worked hard to maintain our standards, did a great job ensuring our clients were happy. Our clients deserved to have a salon they could count on for quality services and a sense of kinship, where they could leave feeling a little bit happier. I also felt our technicians' commitment deserved the same resolve and commitment from us to deliver fruitful business for their hard work. After all, how could we know whether the new owners would be more determined than us, or whether they would treat our technicians fairly and give them the support they needed? Would their focus be to uphold our high standards or to turn a profit?

I'm not sure if I should admit, fortunately or unfortunately, that no one wanted to purchase our growing business, even though we were selling it for a fraction of what it was worth, but I took it as a sign that maybe the business was meant for us after all. After a long period without any buyer interest, I finally decided to be more involved with managing the business behind the scenes and helping with whatever it took to ensure smoother operation. I recognized I had to be more active in this business to help my wife. It took me back to when we had first started the business and what we needed to do.

RECOGNIZING CHALLENGES

When we first started, I recognized the challenges I needed to address when opening a business in Ames, a university town with a population of 58,000. First, I needed to do more research on running a business. This wasn't hard for me, especially with online resources. After all, I had learned to fit into an entirely new culture; I could certainly learn about business. From figuring out a budget to determining whether we had a market and what forms I needed to register with the State, there were many things I needed to gather and maintain. I wanted to make sure the business would not fail because of something simple like neglecting to fill out a form or doing our taxes incorrectly.

Next, as I mentioned before, we knew that Ames already had seven to eight well-established nail salons in different places throughout the community. One of the important keys to the success of a business is choosing the right location. After some time searching for the best options, we found a salon that had four chairs and seemed to be in its final days. This older salon was in the downtown historical train depot. It wasn't what you'd call a perfect location, as it was tucked into a corner at the end of Main Street in a declining downtown area where shopping wasn't first-choice and foot traffic was minimal. That said, the location was central to the town and had sufficient parking space, so we purchased it in 2011 and started our journey.

The next priority involved our service. Like most nail salons, there were limited services, and Anh and I wanted to do something different. Something better. ProNails was unheard of to ninety-nine percent of our current clients. Trust was what we needed to earn, and we knew it would take time. With that in mind, we turned our focus to creating processes and procedures for our services to ensure we earned every client's trust when they stepped foot into ProNails.

We wanted to create a more therapeutic experience with a greater variety of services rather than the usual nail salons that run people through quickly, with TVs and noise coming from every direction. To do this, we decided to design our place with a relaxing atmosphere and soft background music to lighten the spirit. We also added different levels of service for manicures as well as pedicures. Our goal was to deliver a different experience than our competitors—one that would make customers want to come back every time.

In addition to our service, we talked about our next priority—sanitation practices. There was a need for our nail salon to have exceptional sanitary practices to ensure the safety of our customers. It was a priority for both of us. We decided to invest in the Steam Autoclave Sterilizer.

This state-of-the-art equipment was unheard of in Iowa's nail industry in 2011 and the most expensive piece of equipment I purchased. The Steam Autoclave Sterilizer was generally used to sanitize hospital equipment. Our nail salon was one of the first in the industry to purchase and utilize this equipment to ensure that all our customers would have a safe experience.

STAFFING

Recruiting a valuable team of technicians was next on our list. We set up a system to make sure all our technicians were treated fairly and with transparency, especially the newly certified technicians. We opened in February of 2011 and two technicians joined us in August of that year. They are still with us today. Most of our people are like family. They take care of us, and we take care of them. Many have been with us the last four to five years. I'm proud to say our turnover is very low. I'm thankful because it takes a lot of investment to train new employees.

When we trained our employees, we encouraged everyone to say "ProNails" when they were talking about nails to their colleagues, their neighbors, their family, their friends, etc. This was our branding effort to help implement word-of-mouth marketing. It's a valuable strategy to market your business, and more often than not, it's free. If our technicians gave our customers a good experience and talked about ProNails, there was a chance the customers would tell their network of friends. Another strategy our nail salon did was train the technicians to provide a consistent process. If a technician was out when one of their clients needed a manicure or pedicure, then another could step in and provide an equal service and experience.

Over the years, our training and service paid off, and we went from four chairs to eight, and eventually to ten, which is what we have available today. We have clients who will drive two hours one way to see us every two to three weeks. We have other clients in California who visit us every year when they come to Iowa.

On a busy day, we can service more than a hundred customers, but one week, we had to turn away 167 customers. This is good and bad at the same time. While we hate to turn away business, our goal is to provide quality service rather than to rush it. The reason we don't have a lot of walk-in business is because clients are dedicated and schedule their next appointment right away to ensure they get in. I attribute this dedication to quality customer service, professionalism, a friendly atmosphere, and the experience we provide.

In starting, running, and expanding this business, I realized we were successful when we received client feedback like this from Joan, a ProNails customer: "I live in Ankeny but come to Ames to get my nails done and have been coming to you guys for years. I wish that you had a salon in Arizona or Florida for whenever I'm there. You should start a salon there or a franchise and train the people on how you do it here."

This is why we do what we do.

THE HISTORY OF NAIL SALONS

The nail salon industry began well before I was born, of course, but I want to show you its astounding evolution and how customers have changed their mindsets as the industry has shifted. Drawn from a 2018 UCLA study,[3] here is a quick decade-by-decade rundown of all its secrets, challenges, and successes. What's amazing is its unique expansion in the US due in large part to one of Hollywood's favorite actresses at the time:

Starting in the early 1900s, manicures and pedicures were only offered in full-service salons and often were priced and targeted toward wealthy women. The technicians, or manicurists as they were mainly called, were often referred to as "unintelligent gossips and gold diggers." Often, they were also "hypersexualized."

"In the 1920s and '30s, nail polish went into mass production and became available at Five & Dime stores." This allowed for more working-class women to paint their own nails at home. Despite this development, salon service costs continued to be exclusive.

"In the 1950s and '60s, cosmetics manufacturers were developing new colors to mark different seasons." With more choices, there was an influx of women who became interested in well-polished nails, and different classes developed a complex social significance. A manicured hand either marked "well-groomed feminine glamour" or "questionable moral standards," where calmer colors were considered more socially acceptable.

Since the 1970s, due to shifting forces in both technology and migration, salon tools and labor have become less expensive. With the development of the electric file in 1974 and the acrylic nail in 1979, manicures became more affordable and less time-consuming. At the same time, the population of Asian immigrants and refugee women in the US grew due to the global forces of colonialism, war, and changing immigration policy.

Many credit the actress Tippi Hedren with the entry of Vietnamese refugee women into California's nail salon industry.

THE GODMOTHER OF NAILS

Some of you may remember Alfred Hitchcock's *The Birds*, released in 1963. This iconic movie starred Hedren, a talented actress with a beautiful soul. She won a Golden Globe award for her role in that movie, but she had also played in *Marnie* (1964) and made appearances in more than eighty films and shows. Some other well-known films included Charlie Chaplin's *A Countess from Hong Kong* (1967), a satire called *Citizen Ruth* (1996), and the comedy *I Heart Huckabees* in 2004. For these roles and her career, she received the Jules Verne Award and a star on the Hollywood Walk of Fame. She also has a daughter, Melanie Griffith, who you may have seen in several movies, including her Golden Globe-winning performance in *Working Girl* in 1989.

So what does this famous actress have to do with the nail salon industry? According to *Zionsville Magazine*,[4] "the former fashion model and activist had a lot to do with helping Vietnamese refugees get into small nail salons."

In the early days, she began her humanitarian work as an international relief coordinator, helping with the organization Food for the Hungry. In 1975, after the fall of Sai Gon and the takeover of South Viet Nam, Hedren was a volunteer at Hope Village, a refugee camp near Sacramento, California. At 45, she dedicated her time to finding jobs for incoming Vietnamese refugees and brought typists and seamstresses to help train them. There were limited positions they could be trained for, but with the help of twenty Vietnamese women and Hedren, a new opportunity was born—the art of nails.

THE STORY ACCORDING TO NAILS MAGAZINE

In 2015, *NAILS Magazine* published an article titled

"The Vietnamese-American Nail Industry: 40 Years of Legacy."[5] It provides an outstanding summary of how the industry grew with the culture. The catalyst for the story was the reunion of five of the Vietnamese women aided by Hedren after thirty-nine years. In 1975, these women, along with Hedren, completely transformed the American nail industry. Hedren, who served as a volunteer relief coordinator for the charity Food for the Hungry during the Viet Nam War, was instrumental in getting these women licensed.

At a time when the Vietnamese people had to flee their own country to escape persecution and likely death, there were few choices for them. Whether it was meant to be, or the timing was an accident, there couldn't have been a more qualified, connected person than Hedren to help these twenty women in search of the perfect vocation.

One refugee woman, Thuan Le, had met Hedren at Hope Village, the article states. Le could see Hedren was concerned and wanted to help them become independent in America. Le had tried typing and sewing classes, but neither was a good fit for her. Luckily, with the help of translators, Le and other refugee women were able to explain their admiration for Hedren's long, manicured nails, which gave Hedren the idea to train them in the art. Hedren decided to fly in her own personal manicurist along with other trainers to teach the group.

In the article, Kim-Dung Nguyen says, "In my head, I didn't have a picture of what a manicurist was." She was a widowed mother of two young girls, ages six and four. When she arrived at Camp Hope, her English skills allowed her to help coordinators translate training communications between Hedren and the other women. Nguyen expected to be washing dishes upon arrival to the US, but Hedren had given her an opportunity to do something far more fulfilling. Nguyen spread the word, and more women entered the program.

The article explains that after training with Hedren's personal manicurist, Dusty Coots, the women were afforded an unconventional opportunity to finalize their education at Citrus Beauty School in Sacramento, California. Hedren had convinced the school to develop a nails-only program broken out of the the full cosmetology license, allowing the women to focus on what they were most interested in and to begin making money to support their families much faster.

"First they said no, they don't have just a manicure class," Le says in the article, "and it would take years for a cosmetology license. But Tippi convinced them to teach us to do nails only. And the principal accepted us."

The women were required to pass the state board exam in English, and when they did, they received a nail license and went to work.

It is fortunate these immigrants found someone with Hedren's dedication. She was very passionate and determined to find the perfect vocation to match their skills in a way that would allow them to be independent and thrive in this strange, new country they now called home. This original group of twenty women, along with Hedren, played a vital role in the development of an industry now valued at more than $7 billion.

Today, due to the growth of the industry and a higher demand for licensing, many of the industry's veterans have found the opportunity to open schools and teach their own nails-only courses in Vietnamese to many newcomers. Technology and social media have also played a key role in the distribution of knowledge and information among colleagues in the industry worldwide. However, unlike in the early days, many states are now allowing the exam to also be taken in Vietnamese, making it easier for immigrants to roll into the profession shortly after arrival in America.

The article signifies the importance of networking among the Vietnamese and the power it had in growing the industry. According to the article, these twenty refugee women were considered pioneers. Each one of them found positions in salons or opened their own, and soon, word spread to family and friends about how they could also make a good living and become independent in America.

With this boom in the industry, there came a need for more and better supplies. The article mentions Billy Chen Ngo, a refugee among the "second wave of boat people to flee Viet Nam," who sparked the evolution of marketing practices and the beauty supply chain. Before arriving in the US in 1979, Ngo stayed in a Hong Kong refugee camp for eight months. "No one wanted to live under a Communist Regime," he says in the article. "Everyone wanted to find a way out." He attended college for three years, but he still needed a means of survival, and found inspiration in his brother, who had found his way into the nail salon ahead of him.

Ngo purchased photo negatives from Karen's Nail Supply in North Hollywood, the article explains, and had them developed into wall posters, which he sold to nail salons door-to-door out of the back of his van. While on this journey, his clients suggested he sell nippers, nail brushes, and other critical supplies, so he made a deal with Antoine de Paris for nippers, then another with a brush company, another for buffers, then files, and so on, Ngo says in the article. Being the survivalists and opportunists these people were, they expanded upon every opportunity they were presented, and in the mid-1980s, Ngo partnered with Danny Lu and established Starlight Beauty Supply, one of the very few Vietnamese-owned suppliers at the time. A few years later, the article states, they went their separate ways, and he founded yet another company, Skyline Beauty Supply.

Over the years, as opportunities continued to grow, stories like these of more and more immigrants joining the industry in turn attracted more immigrants to the US, which continued to fuel the growth of nail salons and create new opportunities for other entrepreneurs. The industry had become a self-sustaining organism.

Today, demand has changed completely and professionals have had to adapt to this constant change. Before, you had to order supplies from nearby. Your choices were few, and you paid premium prices. In the last decade, technology has allowed the convenience of shopping online and a wider range of suppliers, not confining salons to a particular location in the country. It has also created competitiveness in the market, product innovation, and better customer service, giving the industry the power to demand quality and cost-effective supplies that work for each salon. I remember when we had friends opening salons in Iowa, and we all knew of only one supplier, based in Des Moines. Today, there are scores of large suppliers across the country, most owned by Vietnamese.

Even artificial nail tips and acrylic nail products can be traced to this Vietnamese business boom, according to the article. In the late 1970s, a woman named Mylan Lieng established the first Vietnamese-owned nail manufacturing business, Tru Nails in Reno, Nevada. As demand for acrylic services grew, so did Lieng's business and others like it. Shortly after opening, she moved shop to Garden Grove, California, a location more central to the Vietnamese community. Though Tru Nails no longer exists, the article states, Lieng paved the way for the founding of Nails 2000, currently owned by her sister, Mai Vo.

Their courage, creativity, and entrepreneurial spirits have forged a path for the next generation of Vietnamese-American entrepreneurs who have the desire to contribute to the expansion of the nail industry, giving salon owners more choices when it comes to product selection like iGel Beauty, Chisel, and Joya Mia, all owned by Vietnamese-Americans. Contributions to the nail industry are so vast that the success of entrepreneurs in the US has even reached back home in Viet Nam. Many products like pedicure liners, buffers, files, and gloves are currently being manufactured in Viet Nam. One of many successful brands is Nghia Corporation, a multi-million-dollar company in Viet Nam with a US branch that produces many product lines that specifically serve the American nail industry. Nghia is well-known for their high-quality nippers, clippers, and cuticle trimmers, and it is the preferred brand of many technicians.

As an immigrant, I left Viet Nam and everything I ever knew and loved at my own will, but my story does not compare to the trials and triumphs of this group of individuals. These men and women not only pioneered the nail industry but also gave hope to millions and created new opportunities in the face of extraordinary loss. They endured whatever challenges were thrown at them, never losing faith. They were courageous and determined to succeed in America regardless of what it took, and, in the process, built a legacy that will no doubt support many generations in the years to come.

There is one major difference that I see between the mid-1970s and now. Today, we do nails to build personal success. Back then, they did them purely to survive. This fundamental shift in mindset could not have happened without the struggles these amazing people overcame.

"Hundreds of thousands of harrowing stories of survival through the aftermath of war are the foundation of the Vietnamese community in the US," the article states. In a very real sense, it continues, the fall of Saigon and the end of the Viet Nam War was also the beginning of the Vietnamese nail industry.

As the Vietnamese culture grew in the nail salon industry, so did the need for information and education. *NAILS Magazine* created a sister publication, *VietSALON*

Magazine, in 2006. This publication was geared toward business skills and training as well as health updates on the industry. We have seen our culture grow over the years and have witnessed new information come out each year to aid in its growth. With the opportunities afforded by social media, we are now able to share our best work and offer advice to one another. Nail techs can now inspire one another over the internet. The methods and platforms allowing us to share information have grown drastically, especially in the last decade, and like many other industries, there is now a constant hunger for new information and networking connections to stay relevant.

I appreciate authors who cover not only updates in our industry, but its history and contribution to the evolution of our culture. Their work reminds me of where I came from and the important contributions my culture has provided to our country. As Le states in the *NAILS Magazine* article, "It is thanks to this industry that the first generation could help their families who were left in Viet Nam and raise their children to help them become successful." No doubt many second-generation Vietnamese-American doctors, lawyers, pharmacists, engineers, and business owners owe their success to their parents' hard-earned dollars doing nails, according to the article.

MY REFLECTION

As a successful business owner, I learned so much from this history of my people and the evolution of this industry.

These changes have impacted us in many ways. Vietnamese who want to come to America now have a much easier way to transition. I often think of what it would have been like, coming over to the US with nothing but what you can carry and no connection with anyone, entering a country where you can't even speak the language. I can't imagine these challenges. I came without knowing the language, but I had people to help educate me, and I knew I would be taken care of.

For some, even today, it's still a matter of survival, but at least now they have the education and resources more readily available. They can learn the trade and have a position immediately while they learn English. In addition, the Vietnamese culture has spread throughout the United States and offered a positive influence as opposed to the '70s, when it was only limited to a few locations along the coast and the culture was relatively unknown. Today, people immigrating have more places they can go and still enjoy a community built from their native culture to help them settle in their new home and industry. And we have educational opportunities in Vietnamese, both online and in-person, to provide better training for immigrants while they acclimate to the American culture. I, too, credit Tippi Hedren for beginning all of this.

On the flipside, with the influx of nail salon industries and the wide distribution of services, education sometimes did not meet standards, which resulted in the businesses or salons providing lower quality services. Now, the standard has increased due to the competition, but the service is still undervalued. Take big-chain hair salons, for example. You can go to a cheaper hair salon and get a haircut for $17 pretty much across the board and can expect the work to take fifteen to twenty minutes, but a manicure can range from $35 to $50 for a process that can last up to an hour. But as with any industry, we're continuing to evolve.

Since my people were a major contributor to nail salons, I feel it's my purpose to continue these efforts. I want to educate more about what it was like in the past, what it's like now, and what we can be in the future. This is my contribution—to help others take pride in what they do and help them succeed. We are all fortunate to have opportunities, and turning around to help the next generation is vital to continuing the success for decades to come.

PART 2

Advice for My Fellow Business Owners

So now you have learned about my life. You have seen what I have done to run my own successful nail salon. You have learned the history of my culture and how we became the majority in this industry. None of this was easy. It takes a lot of hard work and dedication to be successful. Vietnamese people are generally hard-working and dedicated, and we tend to regard our families as a high priority and will work hard every day to protect and provide for them.

Unfortunately, one cultural difference I have experienced is that Vietnamese do their work, then go home to their families. American culture tends to emphasize striving to do more, to expand on their original dream. Americans want to grow.

Which perspective is correct? They both are. There is nothing wrong with putting in a hard day of work and going home to your family to spend time with them. My family is the most important thing to me. I also worry that if I don't expand my business and my personal knowledge, I may fall behind, and my business could eventually suffer.

So what do we do?

That's why I wrote this book. Not only to shine the light on how my culture expanded this industry, but to show you how to think about your future in the nail salon industry or any business you aspire to. If you're a technician, a manager, or a business owner seeking ways to become more successful, I want to share what I have learned, teach some important concepts in business ownership, and share some success strategies many have not had the opportunity to learn.

I'm turning away clients because I'm creating an experience they want and will pay more for. If you'd like to know how to do this yourself, then please read on.

WHAT DOES SUCCESS LOOK LIKE?

Have you ever been to a flea market? It's a great place to find good deals, right? Many vendors come in, open their tabletop display, and set up all of their merchandise. They sell throughout the day, then pack everything up and leave.

What are the pros and cons of that scenario? The pros are you don't have a brick-and-mortar building to pay for, you have little need for more employees, and you have little to no maintenance after you close. The cons are you work long hours for little profit. But what if you could double or even triple your hourly pay? What if you could set your own hours? What if you could make more time for your family and even afford to take them on a vacation? What would that kind of success look like to you?

As I've mentioned, family is the most important to me.

For many of us Vietnamese-Americans, we all strive to take care of the people we love. Our culture revolves around working hard and providing safety for them. We were given the opportunity to transition into American culture through the nail salon industry and make an honest wage, but I have realized that in this country, we can still do more, desire more, and become more. We can be successful business owners, but that requires a different kind of education outside of learning the art of nails.

With the influx of Vietnamese refugees coming into America since the early '70s, there were few choices of where to work, but nail salons were a thriving opportunity, and Americans were very accepting of Vietnamese and other Asian refugees doing their nails even though they spoke little to no English. It was a beacon of hope for Vietnamese people to learn that trade and earn money to take care of their families right away while learning the language and culture. We were grateful for the opportunity.

Today, we see many salon owners who have perfected the art of nails but didn't understand the business side of things as deeply because they weren't offered the proper training or skillset. I've seen it too many times in our industry, and the results are failed businesses and worse, dissatisfied customers who receive poor service which reflects poorly on our entire industry. We need to band together and share resources and opportunities so that our industry can survive and continue to thrive. The alternative is we lose our quality of service, then our customers, and finally our livelihoods.

I love my customers and learning about their different backgrounds. They are as different on that side of the table as we are on the other side, holding the nail file. My technicians come from all walks of life. Many are from right here in the heartland, and just as many are not. Regardless, we are all connected, and we work hard to keep our industry thriving.

As I mentioned, I wanted to write this book not only to talk about the history of my culture and my industry, but also to help my colleagues realize their own success story. Opportunities are still out there. These valuable lessons and strategies are imperative to maintaining a successful nail salon industry. I'm going to teach you what you need to consider when you open your own business, what your priorities should be as a start-up, and how to gauge the risk. I'll also speak about advocacy and the importance of having a voice. Finally, I'm going to demonstrate my best practices based on what I've learned as a successful business owner.

One of my favorite quotes is from the late Zig Ziglar, who stated the following: "You can have everything in life you want if you will just help enough other people get what they want."

I have collected several quotes and lessons I have learned over the years, but this one in particular resonates with me the most. You could say I'm a believer in karma, but doing things for others also gives me a sense of fulfillment in my life. So here I am, ready to help anyone interested in business ownership.

WHY EXPLORE BUSINESS OWNERSHIP?

They say the best investment you can make is to invest in yourself. I read a great article from SmallBizGenius.net that supports this idea. It begins with the following: "Small businesses and ambitious enterprises are at the heart of every industry. Not only do they immensely contribute to the overall revenue of a country, but they also have a beneficial effect on the workers themselves.

"Employees who decide to make the switch and become independent employers feel more fulfilled and motivated to work. There are a lot of inspirational entrepreneur statistics out there that show us the US is still the best place in the world to become your own boss and start something new."[6]

The article later states, "It is necessary to understand that the entrepreneurship failure rate has never been lower, with only 22.5 percent of businesses closing after a year.

"With such a promising startup environment, it's no wonder a lot of people are choosing this path over being a traditional employee. For many, entrepreneurship is a great career choice that allows for a better work/life balance and more income.

"Studies have also shown that this is not a young man's game, despite what the public believes. Successful businesses are usually started by middle-aged men and women who have experience and want to apply it in their field."[7]

This article also had some compelling statistics that are great for anyone looking to go into business ownership. First,

64 percent of US billionaires are self-made.[8] That means more than half of the top one percent started out just like everyone else.

It also states that in 2016, 25 million Americans were starting or already running their own businesses and that there are 583 million entrepreneurs in the world. Did you know that more than half—about 60 percent—of small business owners start between the ages of forty and sixty? These are all amazing statistics that support the idea that business ownership is not only achievable but has a great chance of being successful. However, the most important statistic I found was that the number-one reason why businesses fail is that there's no market need.[9] This is something we'll get into later, but it's a very important point when you're considering going into business for yourself.

THE PROS AND CONS OF BUSINESS OWNERSHIP

Much like our discussion of the flea market business, you must evaluate what's important to you when considering the option to open up shop. Most people interested in going into their own business strive to be successful, independent, and flexible enough to spend more time with family, but not everyone in business is doing it for the right reason.

If you're wondering about opening a business or salon, first ask yourself, "Why?" If your goal is simply to make more money, then I'd advise against it. You can make more money being a successful technician working at busy salons. You will endure less risk, enjoy more freedom, and have more time for your family. One of the keys to successful business ownership is the passion you have for the business you want to start. Monetary gain is a short-sighted way of thinking.

If business is your passion, and you desire to disrupt the norm, raise the standard, or simply serve your clients' needs in a way no one else can, then go for it. It's always an advantage to be the one who has a solution to a problem or who finds a need that no one else is serving. This is the foundation of a real business, and we'll examine this concept more closely in the next chapter.

I don't recommend relying on superstition or luck, but it is good to know when to jump at an opportunity and lay out your strategy. Know who your captive audience is and strategize your business to attract and serve the needs of that group.

FUNDAMENTALS OF A BUSINESS STARTUP

I want to offer you a bit more detail on starting your own business. It's important to me to share the lessons I learned the hard way so you can avoid them in the future. Few go through all of these steps and have the education to understand everything that's involved. Many times, the unfortunate outcome is a massive amount of work only to find failure later. Now I'm not saying my strategy guarantees success, but I can give you a solid list of concepts you must learn to give your business startup the best chance it has at success for years to come. To start, let's talk about the importance of your strategy.

LAY OUT YOUR BUSINESS STRATEGY

We've talked about the pros and cons of starting your own business and what you need to consider, and you've decided you want to move forward. What do you need to make a business succeed? The key concept I want you to remember in this entire process is **Solution Thinking**, and it's a long-term process.

Solution Thinking is the process in which you define your problem, then seek answers that are adaptable to change. These solutions are meant to help you move forward in a successful way while also enabling you to pivot in today's ever-changing market and social landscape. Take the pandemic as an example. In 2020, nail salons across the country were faced with shutdowns and the loss of customers almost overnight. They had to adapt to new ways to perform their services for customers to ensure an increased level of safety. Thus, Solution Thinking allowed them to find new ways to keep their businesses open and attractive for customers in a challenging environment. It's your own way of problem solving that allows you to adapt to change. Think of this concept as you define each important step in your business strategy below.

STEP ONE:
CREATE YOUR MISSION STATEMENT AND VALUES

Your mission statement is a short summary of your business' purpose and focus, revealing what the company does, how it does it, and why. It should be simple and concise, short and to the point. Having a mission statement helps you define your company's overall goals and position within your industry for your organization and clients. It also helps your employees have a clear understanding of what they need to do. They can also stay focused on your company's purpose. Having a clear mission statement also sticks out as a reminder of why you're in business.

Values are what generally describe your company's morals, ethics, and ideals, and they also help set a foundation for your organizational culture. I believe values are more important internally than externally because they establish a set of principles and guidance for your employees on how your business operates as a whole. It also gives your clients an insight into what they can expect when doing business with your company and the standards that your business has identified.

Both of these might sound cumbersome for a new small business, but these statements will serve to guide your company as it grows.

STEP TWO:
DETERMINE YOUR TARGET AUDIENCE

Determining your target audience is key to setting up the foundation of your business. Consider the services you may want to offer and the market in the area where you want to start your business. Once you determine what your target audience is, you can further frame your products and services to cater to that demographic. Case in point, you might provide different services to a college crowd than you would a group of retirees. They are at different stages in life and generally have different levels of financial stability and expectations for the service. Not to mention they may be interested in completely different atmospheres, in terms of nail salons.

You must determine who you want to target. Once your target audience is defined, you'll be able to determine how big your market is in the area, and your own unique services.

The next challenge is how you will approach your target audience. How do you find them? Where does this audience go to look for your services? Is it on social media? Is it in the newspaper or radio? Keep these things in mind as you move forward. They don't need to be determined right now, but you will need to address this in the later stages of building your business.

STEP THREE:
RESEARCH YOUR MARKET

Now that you have your target audience determined, it's time to do your research. Who are your competitors? Make a list of all of those in your target.

What do they do? What target audience do they serve? What are their rates? What do they do well and where do they fail?

The last question is particularly important, because where they may struggle, you can possibly excel and provide a better option.

It's not necessary to know what your competitors are doing all the time. Your primary focus will be your own business and what you can do for your own customers. It is good, however, to have this knowledge in the beginning to better understand your market.

Based on this information, you may determine that your target audience prefers one service above others. You may discover that there aren't enough services in this market, or you may find out the market is saturated. In that case, you will have a good idea of the potential you have and the effort you will need to put in to recruit new customers.

Your research will allow you to make better decisions about what you want to focus on. You will be able to find shortfalls in the market and focus on that to grow your business faster. This is your opportunity to differentiate yourself from other businesses in your market.

STEP FOUR:
GET YOUR RESOURCES TOGETHER

In business there are four different representatives you need to work with to establish a foundation. Each carries an important role in starting up and mitigating risk.

#1 – THE BANKER

The banker will help you establish what capital you can acquire through loans to pay for a new location, employees, and other operating funds. This amount will allow you to gauge how much risk you will be taking financially and how much you need to make in the first year and beyond.

#2 – THE CPA (CERTIFIED PUBLIC ACCOUNTANT)

Unless you have a contact that is a certified accountant, you will want to find one and retain their services. They will help you set up your financial infrastructure, identify what tax credits you qualify for, and help you file your taxes and stay in compliance with state and federal laws. You don't have to know all the laws to stay in compliance if you have a good CPA you trust to take care of your business financials. It's imperative that you stay in compliance as any tax violation can bring the IRS to your door with hefty fines that could be detrimental to your business. If you have a good CPA, the risk will fall on them to keep you compliant. It's well worth the investment to retain their services.

#3 – THE INSURANCE AGENT

Insurance can be different for business owners, based on the operation and risk. A good insurance agent with experience in your industry will be key to making sure you have the proper coverage for your operation. They can tell you what's re-quired by law and give you options for anything additional you may want or need to move forward. You will then be able to budget for that on an annual basis.

#4 - THE ATTORNEY

Mitigating risk in your business is key to maintaining security and success. Your attorney can work with you on any contract including loan applications, building contracts, purchasing agreements, and many more to make sure that you aren't missing anything that could hurt your business. They also have the expertise to find protections to add to your contracts that will help you create more opportunities to increase success and/or decrease risk.

With these four representatives involved in your business, you are sure to minimize the violation of any state or federal laws in regard to business. These representatives will give you their expertise and define your options, allowing you to set policies and procedures for your business, but it is up to you to determine which strategies and recommendations to use based on your business model.

STEP FIVE:
FINDING YOUR LOCATION

I've heard, in the business world, that "location, location, location" is the most important strategy when building your company, and it's traditionally great, but I believe "customer service, customer service, customer service" is even more important. As a business leader, word of outstanding service can spread fast, and regardless of your location, people will find you.

So you're armed with a strategy and have an idea of

your target audience. You're well on your way. You now know the potential for your business, but you may still be uncertain whether you should build a brand-new facility (in my case, a salon) or purchase an existing location.

There are advantages and disadvantages to each option, so you want to fully understand the pros and cons of every location you consider. Make sure it matches what's important to you and your market.

Buying a small, run-down business might not seem very grand, but it requires less capital investment up front, allowing you to use the capital for other needs like renovation, marketing, or keeping capital in reserve while you're building your business. It might be a slow business with a small group of followers, but your focus on service and determination to serve them could result in this small group of clients becoming your best salespeople. We did this with our business and started with a handful of clients who brought their friends, family, co-workers, and even their clients to us. People will keep spreading the word of your great service as long as they can see the value you bring to them.

The other option is building a new location, and there is nothing wrong with that if you have a solid business strategy. Often I've seen people build new salons in areas with the least competition and pay high rent for their lease, hoping to monopolize the market in that area. Many do very well until others get the same idea. This is the reason why we see nail salons on every corner in every city and town the US today, disrupting one another's monopolies in hopes that their fancy salon, new equipment, and sense of newness will capture market share. While it is true that if you monopolize the market, you are guaranteed to do well, this only lasts as long as other players aren't entering your market or providing a better service.

Regardless of your location or how many competitors you might have, your business will grow over time as long as you can innovate, change, and adapt to the needs of your clients. This is where you put Solution Thinking into practice. Make sure you continue to understand the needs of your customers. Adapt your services to change, remain relevant, and maintain, if not increase, your customer base.

Building a business is a lot like building a building— one brick at a time, and if you have a strong foundation, then the structure will be stable as it goes up. If you know your target audience, do your market research, and differentiate your services to cater to clients' needs, then your business has a great chance of success.

STEP SIX:
BUILDING YOUR TEAM

Now that you're ready to jump in with both feet, next comes the hard part—getting a team of people on board. They must believe in your business, and it's your job as the team leader to communicate and synchronize everyone's minds to work together to carry out your plan or strategy.

You know what they say: "It's hard to teach an old dog new tricks." Unless you hire people straight out of school, it's hard to get people to change their habits or the process they used at other businesses, but it's important to get everyone on the same page, no matter where they came from or what experience they've had. In the world of nail salons, your technician must be accustomed to your process to give your clients a consistency of experience.

For example, let's say you love a Starbucks caramel latte. You expect that latte to taste the same every time you order it. As a customer, your expectations are set after your first visit. As a business owner, the same applies. Consistency of service ensures customer satisfaction on every visit.

Now that you know the importance of consistency, how do you accomplish this? Simply put, you need to establish uniform training sessions for every new employee so they understand your priorities, goals, business model, and expectations for providing great customer service in your company. The more detail in your training sessions, particularly in the process of each service, the better the outcome of the employee training experience. Your technicians will be left with a thorough understanding of how you want the service to be provided to your customer. I encourage any team-building exercises and relationship-building practices to be added to your detailed training sessions. Together, you become a single, effective team rather than a collection of individuals.

In addition, keep in mind that you must base your training sessions on the priorities of your business model. I could give you the complete training I give my technicians, but my training might not focus on your priorities. Once you have those determined, you can create the best education for your technicians that will directly provide a clear path to success. Another important part of team-building is developing culture. Having a strong business culture helps establish an environment that unites the team behind a sense of the work they are doing, the values they believe in, and how to get there. In a team, strong bonds encourage communication and collaboration between members to effectively pursue the company's goals and stay focused on the company's vision. I believe a great culture attracts and retains your top talent. It also encourages employee engagement, which drives up productivity and performance that can equate to more profit for the company.

Nothing done right can be done overnight, so if you continue to set expectations for your employees and embody those practices every day as a leader, you set a great example for the rest to follow. Reinforce the right behavior and recognize those who embrace the company culture as you would with any other aspect of work. People can't fix what they don't know, so make sure you provide constructive, honest feedback often that can lead to a healthy business culture.

Having the right team members and a positive culture can be a tremendous force for your company, so to fuel your growth, don't underestimate the importance of curating your talent and building a culture that attracts and retains it.

STEP SEVEN:
ESTABLISH VALUE

The key consideration in customer retention is building value into each service and product. Create a process and procedure for each of your services in your own way, whether that means focusing on uniqueness, quality, or both. In the nail salon business, your services will need to cater to your clients' well-being as the top priority, ensuring maximum enjoyment and quality of service without degrading the health of their nails. For example, you can offer a sugar scrub, a therapeutic mask with rejuvenation properties, or a paraffin wax treatment to soften heels. And for clients with weak, brittle nails, you can use products to strengthen them over time like a powder dip. For clients who love the elegance of artificial nails, then you must be mindful not to thin their nails too much in the process and instead focus on strengthening their natural nails so that they have more options should they desire a different product or service. Whatever the ser-vices you might offer, the priority should be providing beautiful, healthy nails.

If you're going into business in a different industry, apply this concept in your own way. Find out what will help the client the most and provide that service in a safe and efficient manner.

When providing such services as a nail salon does, beauty is usually what the clients seek, but safety and well-being must also be regarded. You must also seek through your processes and procedures to minimize the risk of bacterial contaminations, create a process to properly sterilize your tools, equipment, and pedicure tubs as well as the entire workspace, and ensure your technicians follow every step of the required procedure. This safety net can be the lifeline of your business. We have seen many salons fail due to lawsuits and bad publicity through news outlets or social media. Eliminating all risks is impossible, but as a business owner, one of your top priorities is to minimize that risk as much as you can. Go above and beyond what your state requires, and your clients will appreciate your business that much more.

STEP EIGHT:
RELATIONSHIP BUILDING

The nail business can be seasonal, and if you're focused on building a fast food-type business or live in a touristy city where repeat customers do not exist, building relationships might not seem very important, but keep in mind that giving your clients an experience that makes them feel connected after they leave is still a great value to hold. Again, tourists talk to other tourists, and many look for recommendations when they are visiting because they don't know the area.

Even if you find yourself in this kind of market, you can still build a repeat client base that will help your business in the slow season. As you might know, retaining a customer is cheaper and easier than acquiring a new one, and building a friendship with your clients not only strengthens the relationship, but can also result in them promoting your business to their friends, family, co-workers, colleagues, and social media connections.

I'm not saying you should wine and dine them, but building a friendship with everyone coming through your door is always beneficial. Get to know them and greet them by name. You can even find out their favorite nail color so you make sure you have it on hand when they visit. After all, you have an hour of opportunity for small talk, to learn about their hobbies and what gets them excited, and to ask about their kids and/or grandkids. The majority of people like to share their life experiences, personal stories, and vice versa. They'd also like to get to know you, so don't be shy. It will make the work go by faster, and it will be far more interesting. Not every client will want to chit-chat, and you'll have some who just want to relax, but make sure to learn at least what they like and how they want to be served.

Think of it this way. You aren't in the business of doing nails; you're in the business of customer service, and you need to know your clients to better serve them. We're living in a busy world with less and less face-to-face interaction. When clients come to get their nails done, they appreciate the interactions and conversations. If you can make the service more than just a nail service, alleviate their stress, create laughter, and make them happier when they leave than when they came in, then you've created an experience your clients will always look forward to.

STEP NINE:
ADAPT TO CHANGE

As I mentioned in the introduction, Solution Thinking is a key concept to use every day you are in business. Having the ability to make decisions that can address the ever-changing business environment can determine your success rate. Let's look at one example.

In 2020, the pandemic definitely threw a curve ball to a lot of businesses, and we were no exception. We were shut down for almost two months, uncertain of when we might be able to re-open as we witnessed cases continue to rise and news outlets keeping track of death rates across the nation. It was scary, but it wasn't the virus that scared us; it was the uncertain state of the economy and whether we would be able to re-open for business again. We were completely unaware of what was going to happen next, whether people would be comfortable going out in public when we re-opened, or whether the sluggish economy would put people in a tighter budget so that getting nails done was no longer a priority. Our biggest worry revolved around the technicians who relied on us to provide them with work, so we were even more determined to prepare for re-opening.

I've long believed that our salon doesn't need additional air circulation as most of our products are organic and non–toxic compared to what was commonly used in the industry in the past. I would go so far as to say, if you're blindfolded, walking into our salon, you wouldn't be able to tell it's a nail salon. However, we proceeded with the installation of an air circulation system that we had planned to install long before the COVID–19 pandemic. The system was designed to pull air from every station and pedicure chair, creating a down draft air curtain between technicians and clients, effectively removing contaminated air from our space better than any glass divider commonly seen in other businesses.

The project took a while, but luckily, it was completed right before the State of Iowa allowed businesses to re-open. To ensure the safety of our technicians and clients, we implemented a mask mandate for our salon. When there was no statewide requirement, we asked our clients not to come into the salon until their scheduled time to allow a smoother transition of people coming and going and to minimize overcrowding of our common area. There was no more signing in, and we also asked every client to wash their hands prior to selecting their favorite polishes and spaced people out as much as possible. Cleaning and disinfecting have been a norm for us, but we ramped up and disinfected all surfaces at each station after every client.

After we re-opened from the state-wide shutdown, we continued to have support from our regular clients, even though it was nowhere near our regular crowd, but it was better than we expected because of our reputation for all the extra safety precautions we had always taken. In addition, our ability to continue implementing safety measures and to adapt to different environments helped earn their trust. They would tell us ProNails Spa and the grocery store were the only places they would venture out to during this time. It was our clear message that our business was doing something right.

It appeared most of our clients were ready and happy to receive vaccinations when they became available, and we were seeing more and more familiar faces return and tell us that one of the first places they wanted to go to after they'd gotten their shots was ProNails.

We learned many great lessons facing this pandemic, and our business used Solution Thinking to pivot and adapt to overcome our challenges. As a result, we recovered well and are now thriving again. We were glad to see our clients coming back, and not just for their business, but we were glad to provide them with an experience they enjoy. This pandemic proved that we had earned their trust, which meant the world to us. As our slogan says, "We truly enjoy your presence," and we mean it.

THE IMPACT OF BUSINESS AND INDUSTRY

It's easy to go through life without pausing to think about the little things. As a result, we don't realize the impact small details can have on people and businesses. We buy our groceries at the local market, pump our gas at the most convenient station, and go to the same family doctor for years. Without thinking, we are contributing to the success of these individuals and industries, allowing them to innovate, produce goods more efficiently, and provide a stable career for everyone involved.

Your simple visit to the nail salon supports the non-essential nail industry that has improved the lives of many generations of people beyond the wildest expectations they might have had in their own native country. I'm not sure how many have come to the realization that their visits to nail salons have provided so many the opportunity to live their dream, the American dream.

As an immigrant, I know how my life would have been had I stayed in Viet Nam. The opportunities would have been limited, and the chances to succeed would have been slim. I probably would have had to hustle from dawn to dusk every single day to put food on the table, but here in the US, we own our own business, a home, vehicles, and most importantly, our own happiness.

For many years, the nail industry has been a bridge for immigrants, especially the Vietnamese, to adjust to a new life overseas. When they arrive here, this industry allows them to live within their comfort zone, working alongside colleagues who speak their native tongue. More importantly, it allows them to start building their new lives and be more confident in a new culture.

When you consider starting your own business, be mindful that you are joining a bigger picture here. You will be a part of an entire industry you can contribute to. On the flip side, you can also hurt the industry if you fail to provide products and services that the industry expects. As you look at all these options and make your decision about how to move forward, keep your mind open and always be aware that you have colleagues in the industry who can be helpful. Having the opportunity to own your own business is great, but joining an industry and having a network of people with the same interests whom you can learn from is priceless. Don't be afraid to network with other professionals and offer your help to them. If you're serving a different area and/or clientele, there is no reason why you shouldn't share what you know to help other non-competing businesses contribute to the industry.

The growth of the nail salon industry into a $7 billion empire is a direct result of people sharing ideas, learning the trade, and helping others succeed. That said, you have a responsibility to help protect that industry as well.

As I mentioned before, we made many changes to keep our customers safe during the pandemic. We recognized that we must set a good example for our fellow businesses and community, sending a message that they are important to us. In the industry, we are always faced with challenges. I urge you to consider setting a good example in your community by running a good business, being involved in your community, and also standing up when challenges arise. For nail salons, most of our challenges, outside of economic fluctuation, occur when laws are created that hinder the successful practice of our trade. Each industry needs strong advocates in the legislature to protect it from increased regulatory burdens, or as I would say, the creation of too many laws that hinder our business practices. This is one of the more challenging, yet important aspects of business and one that I recommend you take part in after you're more established and comfortable speaking about your experience.

WHAT IS ADVOCACY, AND WHY IS IT IMPORTANT?

Many of us in the industry know about the importance

of having a voice when it comes to new laws, but few have any true understanding of how the process works. We as members of the industry need to educate lawmakers on which laws help (and hinder) our industry's future, and which laws keep our customers, employees, and environment safe without overreaching. This is done through advocacy, which is defined as public support for, or recommendation of, a particular cause or policy.

For those of us who have lived in Viet Nam first, we have experienced a socialist government. For those of you born and raised here, I hope some of my book has helped you see the difference between socialism and democracy, which is the foundation of the US government. There are pros and cons to both, but here I want to emphasize the importance of advocacy and why we need more of it. Let me tell you a story about a time when the government's lack of understanding and education directly affected the nail salon industry.

As I mentioned before, the pandemic burned through the world, and we had to change the way we conducted our business almost overnight. Governor Gavin Newsom of California stated in a press conference that the first case of COVID-19 started in a nail salon, and in a matter of hours, customers began shunning nail salon businesses across America in fear of catching COVID-19. As a result, Governor Newsom shut down salons across the state, and they were among the last to be able to re-open. Hair salons, restaurants, and other businesses were all able to re-open before nail salons. The primary reason was the lack of education Governor Newsom had about how nail salons work, and his ignorance created huge hardships and challenges for thousands of business owners. Many nail salons did not survive this blunt and misinformed accusation.

How do we avoid unfortunate incidents like this moving forward? The answer is simple. We need to talk to our legislative leaders and make sure they understand how we work, what we contribute to the economy, and how important we are as an industry. But many of us may feel too intimidated to talk to our leaders or may not know how to educate them. So how do we become an effective voice for our business?

One answer is to get involved with state and national organizations that already represent your industry. This is a great strategy for anyone looking to be a business owner. For me, the National Nail Association of America (nnaa.org) is a national nonprofit organization with a mission statement that declares, "Coming together to strengthen our position within the industry." They gather information and maintain a network of nail salon industry leaders, allowing them to communicate with and learn from one another for the purpose of educating policy-makers on important topics like business operations, current laws, and marketing strategies. When you become a member of an organization like this, you gain access to a great deal of information and increase your network with like-minded leaders who can help you. You also make a difference in educating our legislative leaders to create constructive, and not destructive, laws. Now, more than ever, we need to have a strong voice and a great message to offer our legislators. This is what organizations like the

NNAA can help provide.

Organizations that can assist with your industry exist at both the state and local level, but either way, I would recommend getting involved when you're ready. One of the best things about being in this business is knowing that I'm a part of something bigger than myself. I'm making an impact, providing for my family and others in my business, and I'm representing an industry that has helped my culture survive and thrive in the United States for many decades. It's my American dream and one that I'm proud of.

FINAL WORDS OF WISDOM

Now you know my journey from the banks of the Perfume River in Viet Nam to a successful nail salon in Ames, Iowa. This road has had unexpected curves and bumps along the way—more than many have dealt with in life—but I'm proud of my native heritage, my new heritage, my industry, and the choices I've made that led me to living the American dream. I'll never forget my roots or my wings, and I encourage everyone to do the same.

My family is stronger because of what we went through together, and I'm proud of what we have accomplished. I feel it's my duty to share what I have learned with other aspiring business owners and leaders. Whether you're in the nail salon industry or something completely different, I want you to take in all that I have to offer in this book and make your own choices. Don't be afraid of the challenges that will inevitably come, but instead examine each one and work with your team using Solution Thinking.

As I mentioned earlier, passion is one of the keys to successful business ownership. More than anything, you must be passionate about your business. You also must have perseverance and be able to motivate yourself to tackle challenges and move forward. As a result, your business will not only succeed, but thrive for years to come.

I know I have given you a lot of great information to start your own business, and it can be overwhelming when seriously considering opening shop, but take each concept one step, and one day, at a time. Each decision you make and challenge you overcome will get you one step closer to success in a business you can be proud of.

Be willing to learn, always. There are new strategies and new technologies that make business operations and practices easier. Take everything into consideration as you move forward. You learn much more with an open mind and the willingness to explore better practices as they develop.

Keep your team trained well and up to date on the latest policies. This will also maintain consistency in your business, a key value for your clients.

Finally, don't get discouraged by small challenges. Many people out there in the world don't have the opportunity to own a business. Look at your challenges and obstacles as opportunities to grow and learn something new. It will keep you motivated, and once you find your solutions, you will feel a sense of accomplishment.

Now it's my turn to help others who have the same goals and dreams. If you're a nail technician, or someone who has dreamed of becoming a business owner, I hope you have found this little book helpful. For more information and resources, please review the Index. For questions about my story and how to learn more, please feel free to email me at biayers.polished@gmail.com.

I wish you the best of luck in your endeavors, and don't give up on your dreams. They are within reach.

The ProNails team in 2022.

REFERENCES

1. "Vietnamese Contributions Did You Know?," *International Focus Magazine*, February 16, 2019, https://ifmagazine.net/vietnamese-contributions-did-you-know

2. Georgia McIntyre, "What Percentage of Small Businesses Fail? (And Other Need-to-Know Stats)," last updated 20 Nov 2020, https://www.fundera.com/blog/what-percentage-of-small-businesses-fail

3. UCLA Labor Center, "Nail Files: A Study of Nail Salon Workers and Industry in the United States," November 2018, https://www.labor.ucla.edu/wp-content/uploads/2018/11/NAILFILES_FINAL.pdf

4. Janelle Morrison, "Tippi Hedren: The Godmother of the Vietnamese Nail Industry," *Zionsville Magazine*, December 2019, https://zionsville-monthlymagazine.com/tippi-hedren-the-godmother-of-the-vietnamese-nail-industry

5. Kimberly Pham. "The Vietnamese-American Nail Industry: 40 Years of Legacy," *NAILS Magazine*, December 2015, https://www.nailsmag.com/381867/the-vietnamese-american-nail-industry-40-years-of-legacy

6. Dragomir Simovic, "38 Entrepreneur Statistics You Need to Know in 2022," SmallBizGenius.com, February 2022, https://www.smallbizgenius.net/by-the-numbers/entrepreneur-statistics/#gref

7. Ibid.

8. Ibid.

9. Ibid.